MY FIRST GUJARATI WORDS BOOK

Learn Gujarati in English

PICTURE BOOK

Shalu Sharma

SAPHARAJAN
સફરજન – APPLE

BATAKANI
બટાકાની –
POTATO

PHOOL ફૂલ –
FLOWER

PUSTAK पुस्तक – BOOK

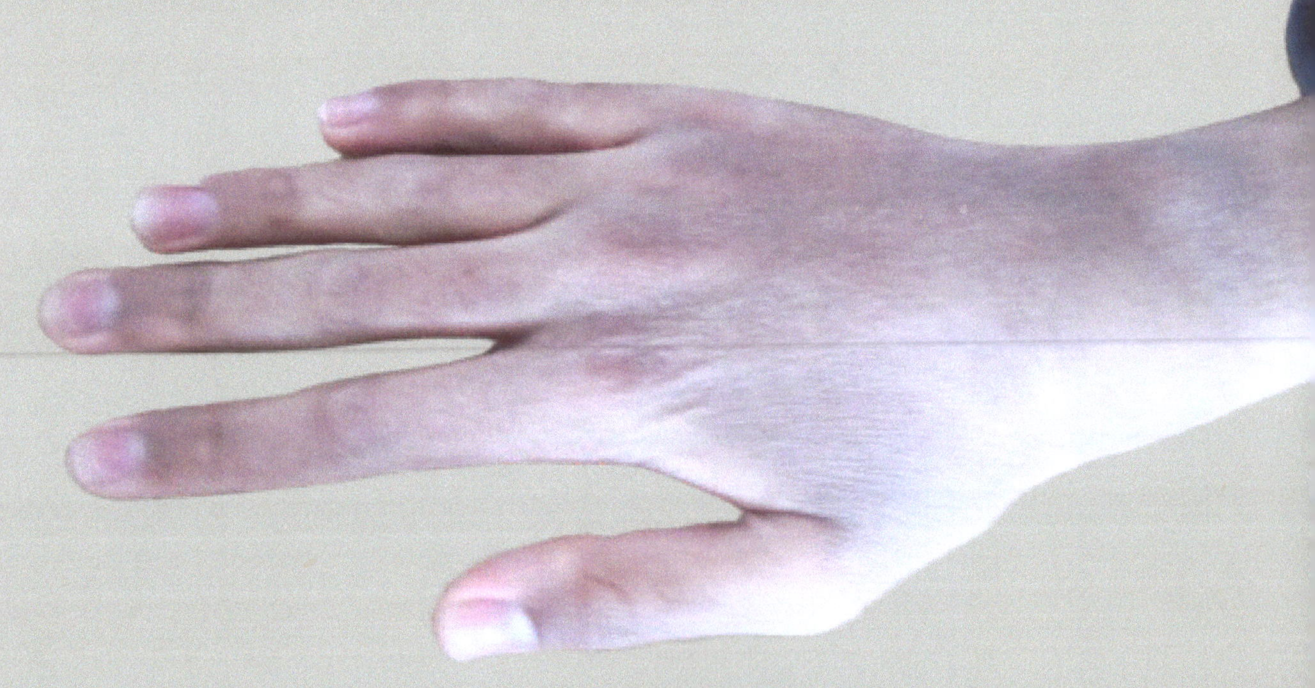
HAATH હાથ –
HAND

DADO εsὶ – BALL

GHADIYAL
ઘડિયાળ – CLOCK

KEDA કેળા –
BANANA

INDA ఈడి –
EGG

GHAR ઘર - HOUSE

MOM મોં – MOUTH

CHASMA
ચશ્મા –
GLASSES

CHODWO છોડવો – PLANT

DOODH दूध – MILK

PAANI પાણી – WATER

SABU સાબુ – SOAP

TOPI ટોપી – CAP

MOTORCAR
મોટરગાડી – CAR

DRAKS દ્રાક્ષ
– GRAPES

PADACHAYO

પડછાયો – SHADOW

VAL વાળ – HAIR

AANKHO
આંખો - EYES

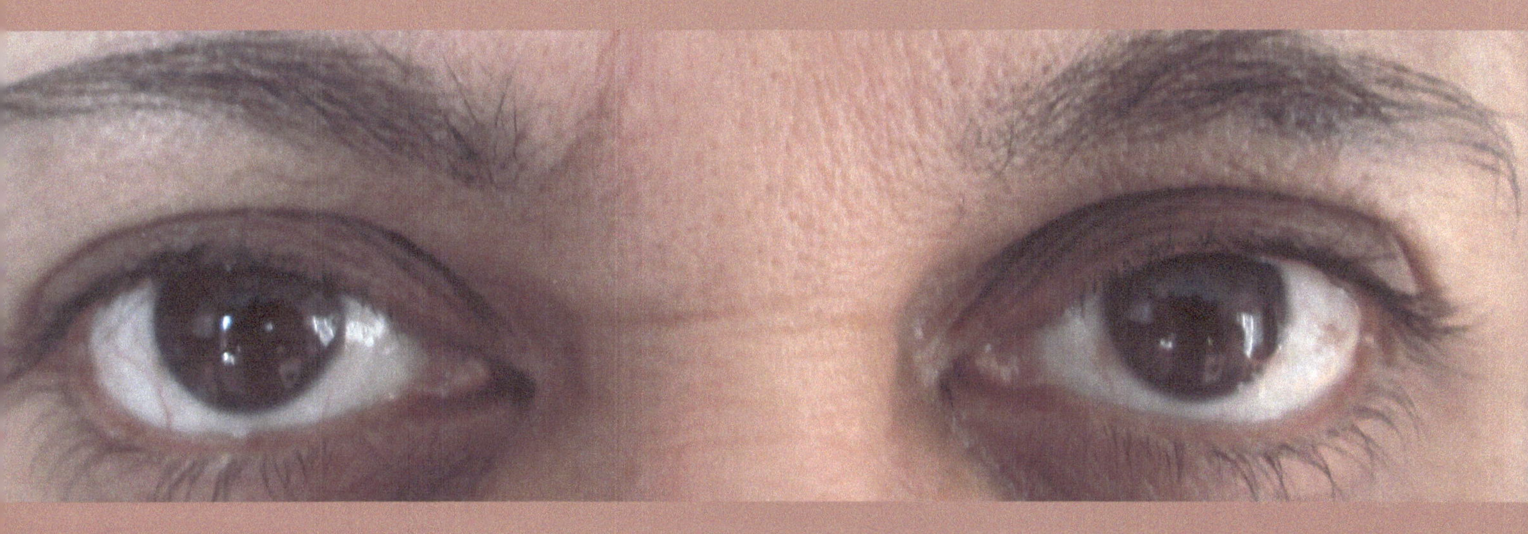

VRRKSA વૃક્ષ
– TREE

KHORAK ખોરાક – FOOD

NAAK નાક –
NOSE

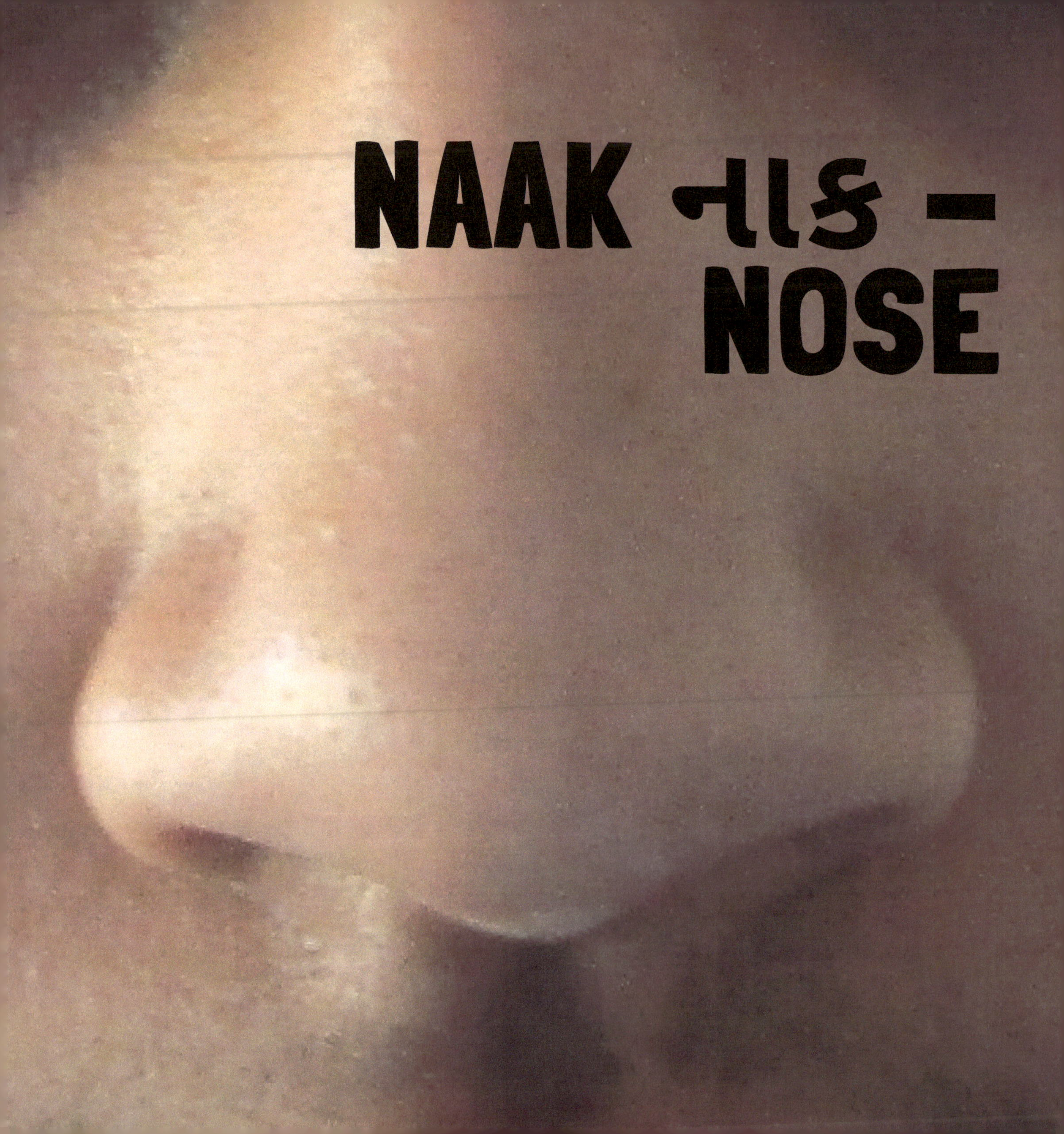

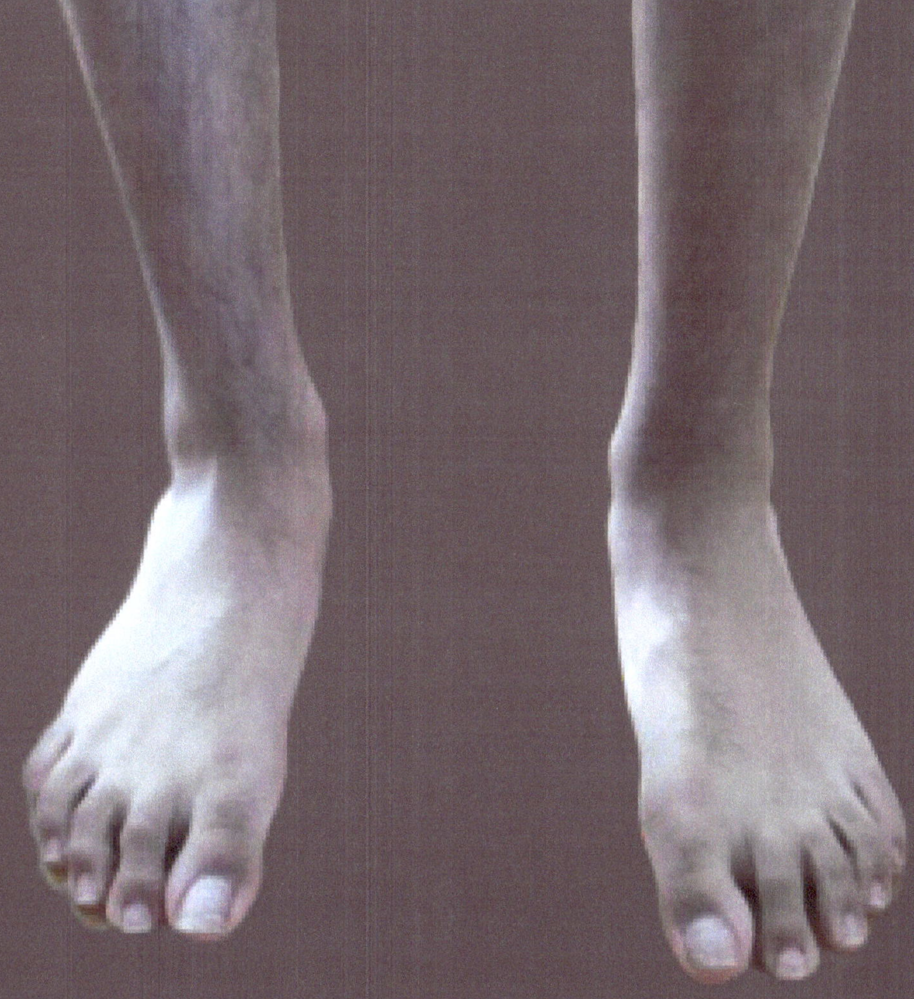

PAG પગ – LEG

KUTARO
ફૂતરો – DOG

PARN
LEAF
પર્ણ—

KHURASI ખુરશી - CHAIR

BILADI
બિલાડી -
CAT